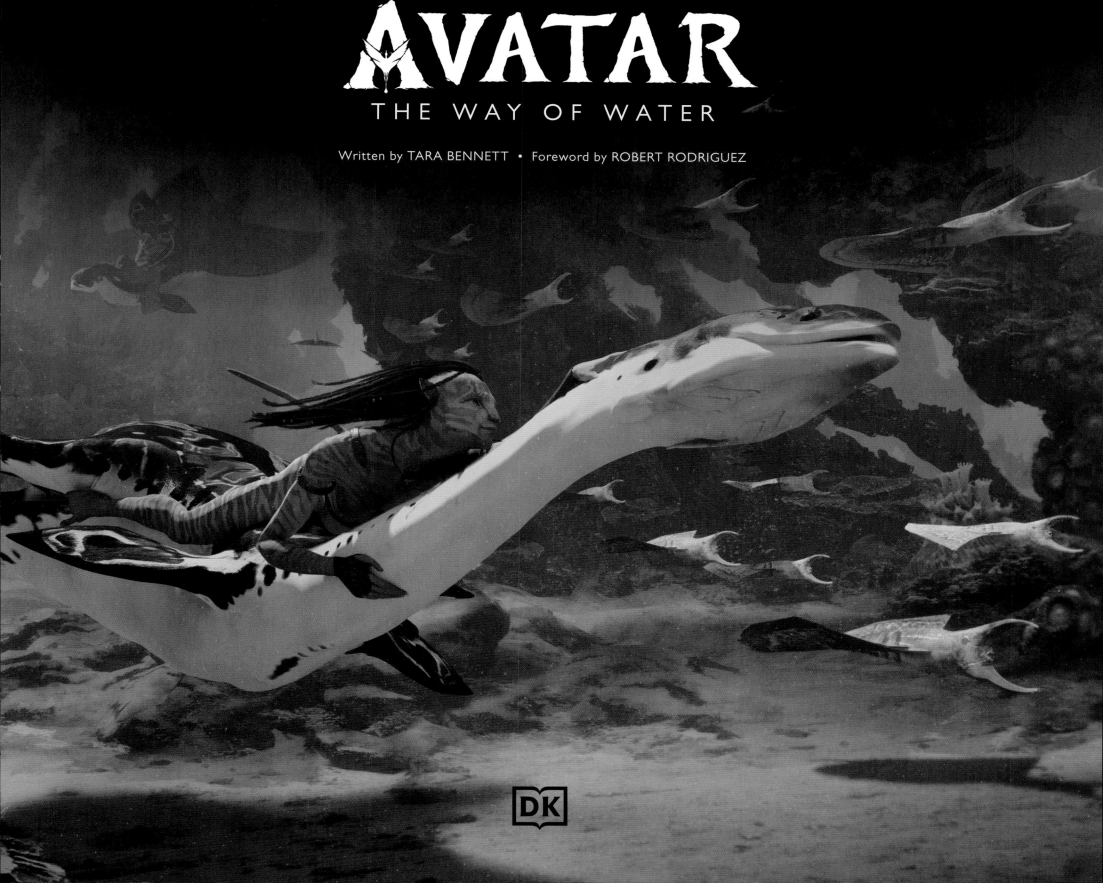

AVATAR
THE WAY OF WATER

Written by TARA BENNETT • Foreword by ROBERT RODRIGUEZ

DK

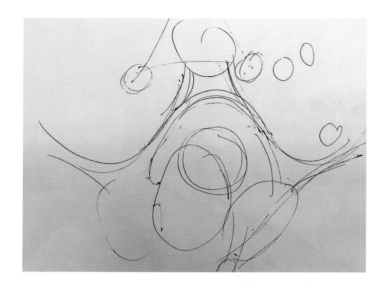

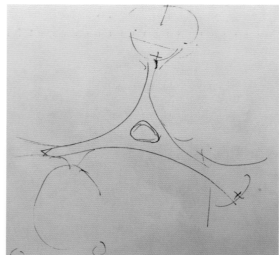

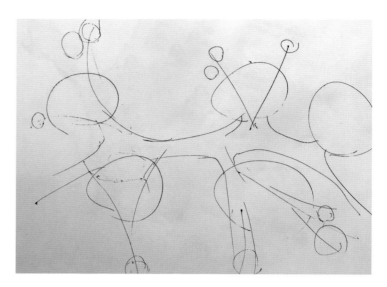

Equipped with their unique skill sets and experiences from *Avatar*, the pair note that those early days on the sequels were all about connecting to both Cameron's broad-stroke and granular ideas. While there were no formal scripts to work from, Cameron provided Procter and Cole with lists of characters and settings. Together with Landau, the four would sit in a conference room as Cameron verbally explained the major set pieces and concepts integral to his vision of the sequels.

Cameron remembers the initial conceptual needs he gave to the designers: "We need the reef village. We need the coral reef. We need the apex predator, which was the *akula*. We need the social and more benign dolphin-equivalent metaphor. And then we have the scarier, warrior mount, the skimwing. I knew that I wanted there to be, essentially, a giant flying fish. But you could interpret that in many, many ways. I knew there was going to be a wing-in-ground-effect ship that was essentially the bad guys' ship. So all of the categories and the subjects existed. We just had no idea what they looked like.

"Everybody thinks that I come to it with this sort of crystal clarity. But that's not the case at all," Cameron admits with candor. "It's like having 500/20 vision where you see some big, blurry thing, but then your vision just gets better and better and better as you go along. It's all about bringing these ideas into finite focus. It's a highly collaborative, highly iterative process that requires an awful lot of talking. You draw. You paint. You talk. Then you look at it."

That process taught Cole and Procter how to translate Cameron's intentions into a cohesive design system. "We didn't start at the start, so to speak," Procter explains, "but that led to the insight, as opposed to the example."

Procter says he came to understand that Cameron works in visual metaphors, which in turn needed to be incorporated into the strategies of both design teams. "There needs to be a symbolism to our designs that evokes some emotional response in the audience," Procter details. "It gives a context to how something belongs in the story because it reminds you of something that has its own history attached to it. It's not enough for something just to look cool. It's got to have all these little neurons firing that remind you of other stuff."

AVATAR AESTHETICS

As a populist filmmaker, Cameron imparted to the team that his design ethos in film was all about achieving immediate audience recognition. "Jim, as a filmmaker, really dons that hat, even when he's thinking about individual shots, or the framing of shots, and how long he holds a shot," Procter assesses. "How long do a person's eyes take to recognize what they're looking at, and then recognize the emotion it evokes so that you can then cut to the next shot? He's looking for design to play its own role in that process, in the sense that things need to read clearly, both in terms of design and how your eye can understand it."

OPPOSITE, TOP ROW: **Reef village sketches** | James Cameron
OPPOSITE, BOTTOM: **Reef village concept** | David Levy

ABOVE: **Skimwing concept** | Zach Berger

OVERLEAF: **Bioluminescent reef concept** | Dylan Cole

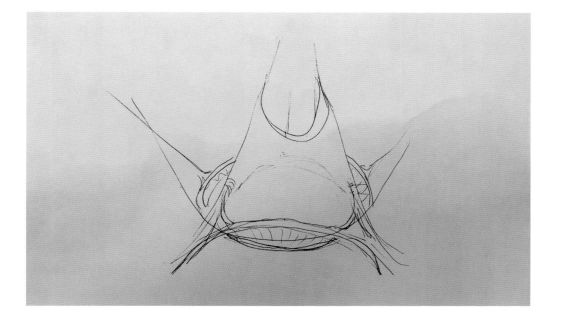

Over the design development for *Avatar: The Way of Water* and the other forthcoming sequels, production designers Dylan Cole and Ben Procter and costume designer Deborah L. Scott, along with their teams, have generated thousands of pieces of concept art, creature and character studies, and texture and textile sketches. Not to mention countless functional physical samples for production including costumes, props, and maquettes. The volume of output from the department heads and their teams is staggering.

"The challenge for the production and costume designers was greater than first met the eye," says Landau. "They not only had to design the sets, characters, and creatures, but they needed to create every single bit of set dressing, every prop, every piece of jewelry, and so on. The task was immense."

How, then, do you collect all of that creative output—the ideas used and the ones left behind—within the finite pages of this book? It is impossible. However, what does emerge from the mountain of conceptual challenges presented to Cole, Procter, and Scott by director James Cameron are some very specific creations from all three teams that have come to quintessentially represent *A2*'s unique aesthetic.

This chapter drills down into those particular design challenges from each team. The department heads identify why each required so much research, conceptual studies, and alternative explorations. They then detail how the art became essential in establishing signature aesthetics that would in turn help define overall looks for their departments. These keystone pieces then went on to inspire the direction and parameters of countless other designs explored in subsequent chapters.

Because of the ambition of *A2*'s narrative, just about everything created for the sequel was done so from scratch. While *Avatar*

established much in terms of the Na'vi mythology, biology, and culture, Cameron was not interested in repeating what they had already done. As such, in this first sequel, he planned to only tease at the familiar flora and fauna of the lush rain forest inhabited by the Omatikaya and instead focus on transporting audiences to altogether new terrain. Gone would be the green of Pandora's forest, supplanted with the gorgeous jewel-tone blues of the ocean-based habitat of the Metkayina and their surrounding environs.

In space and on Earth, the RDA have been busy for the last 14 years as well, evolving their technology to manufacture their ever-expanding arsenal of aircraft, ocean vessels, machines, and mining devices used to pillage Pandora. They also introduce Recom soldiers, outfitted by the RDA for all-out warfare, brought to the moon's surface to stop Jake Sully (Sam Worthington), Neytiri (Zoe Saldana), and their family from interfering with the RDA's corporate goals.

Every creation has a story, and Cole, Procter, and Scott each had to traverse their own exacting design hurdles. Translating the Pandora in James Cameron's head onto the screen in the most dynamic and awe-inspiring ways was their primary and unified goal.

It became clear that for each creative team, particular concepts would become essential in determining a look, technique, or aesthetic that would ultimately become foundational to the story, characters, or landscapes. Figuring out those design conundrums to get the most effective results would in turn inform all of the explorations featured in these pages. From these studies came a wellspring of ideas that Cameron would personally comment on, adjust, and then approve. Consequently, these final forms would provide roadmaps through which each department would elevate the visual story and bring Pandora to newfound heights.

OPPOSITE, LEFT: **Ronal funeral costume concept** | Wētā Workshop
TOP LEFT: **Bridgehead NeuroLab concept** | Shari Ratliff, Jonathan Berube, Steven Messing
LEFT: **Bioluminescent beach at night concept** | Dylan Cole
ABOVE: **Omatikaya village sketch** | James Cameron

PANDORAN DESIGN TEAM

"I was working with the concept artist team to come up with what a marui is. What is a walkway? While they were refining details and structures, I was working with the Lab, moving around all the pieces and trying to come up with good sight lines and a general layout. Since the beginning, the general layout of the village more or less stayed the same. It's a large U-shape, with the commons in the middle and two big arms of mangroves going around it, one side over sand, the other over the water."

—DYLAN COLE

WITH ONLY A FRACTION of Pandora's expansive biodiversity revealed to audiences in *Avatar*, Dylan Cole and his team of concept, character, and creature designers were tasked with introducing an entirely new biome in *Avatar: The Way of Water*—the world of the Metkayina. As reef-dwellers, they exist in a community built over water in a series of interconnected *maruis*, or suspended woven dwellings. Dubbed "reef village" by Cameron, the director explained and sketched its general aesthetic and shape language on a whiteboard for Cole in their very first deep-dive meeting for the sequels.

Citing architect and designer Richard Buckminster Fuller's concept of Dymaxion design, which uses the "maximum gain of advantage from minimal energy input" to influence a shape, Cameron challenged Cole to figure out the composition of the Metkayina's specific architecture: "I said, 'You're building tensile structures and woven structures that are formed within. Let nature be your architect.'" Cameron's sketches and his design brief became Cole's starting point. And because of its importance, the finished look remained an elusive concept that took three years to lock down.

RIGHT: Metkayina village concept | Dylan Cole

NEYTIRI—NEW WARDROBE

One particular composition she was asked to design was an Omatikayan chest piece for Neytiri that Scott describes as looking like a bone sculpture augmented with leaves. "That piece went through what felt like a billion iterations," she shares. "Trying to figure out how the heck to build it was really hard. It imparts strength, but it is also a very delicate piece, both organic and alien." Scott says Cameron's immediate impression was that the piece made her look regal, which was what he wanted it to accomplish. Scott adds, "His words guided me to an essential theme that has helped to define all the designs. Each piece needs to be unique, something you have never seen before, something you can't quite identify, yet it remains beautiful."

TOP: Plant wing print concept | Keith Christensen

ABOVE: Neytiri neckpiece concept | Keith Christensen

RIGHT COLUMN: Neytiri pectoral leaf concepts | Keith Christensen

OPPOSITE, LEFT: Neytiri neckpiece photo | Wētā Workshop

OPPOSITE, RIGHT: Neytiri final look | Keith Christensen, Wētā Workshop

RONAL'S LOOK

The Metkayina costuming not only distinguishes them from the Omatikaya and their aesthetics, but every piece they wear is also a visual extension of their personalities and culture. Establishing a look for the new clan members was a huge undertaking for Scott and her team, but two character looks in particular ended up clearing the design path for a myriad of costuming choices going forward.

Ronal (Kate Winslet) is the chieftess and *tsahìk* of the Metkayina clan and has a sizable personality that is exhibited in her walk, her clothes, and her adornments. As one of the first costumes they designed and manufactured for any character, Scott says it represents the variety of sourcing used to bring a new people entirely foreign to audiences to life.

"One of the core things that I think about when I'm creating a new costume is the circumstances under which it will be worn and how that will affect the motion, the sound, and things like that," she explains.

For Ronal's intricate top, woven with shells, Scott says the idea came from beachcombing in New Zealand. "Beautiful things wash up on the shore all the time, like pieces of shell, wood, plant life, all different shapes, colors, combining to make unique forms." She collected a shell with a cylindrical shape that almost felt fabricated, but it was totally natural. "I went into Wētā Workshop and together with the artisans created the concept for that pāua top. Each one of those shells is individually carved and arranged on a woven framework."

Scott says it was also decided that no one else would wear a skirt but Ronal, which makes her even more distinguished. "On the skirt, there are mixes of different kinds of shells. And that lavender color is from shells that I picked up on the beach. We went back in and made our own versions of the shells with 3D printing. And as for the other skirt, when you first see her in the film, the color is very vibrant. It's prideful. It's elaborate. You see her coming. When we first see her in the movie, she parts the crowd, and with the color and the movement of the costume, everyone is like, 'Oh, who's that? That must be somebody important.'"

BELOW LEFT: Ronal golden collar concept | Wētā Workshop
BELOW MIDDLE: Ronal skirt, full dress photo | Wētā Workshop
BELOW: Ronal seaweed skirt concept | Keith Christensen

OPPOSITE, LEFT: Ronal seaweed skirt concept | Wētā Workshop
OPPOSITE, TOP RIGHT: Pāua cascade top sample | Wētā Workshop
OPPOSITE, BOTTOM RIGHT: Ronal seaweed skirt photo | Wētā Workshop

BIOLUMINESCENCE

Another returning visual component from the first film into this sequel is organic bioluminescence. This time it is seen underwater and casts the creatures and coral with an even more otherworldly feel and a broader color palette. The phenomenon is heightened by the eclipse season, a very specific event that spurred Dylan Cole and his team to figure out the rules of when and how the biolume is seen. "It led to a lot of questions, like is it a function of an amount of light? Or are they actually on some sort of diurnal, circadian rhythm-type thing where they know to wake up at certain times?" Cole says. "Of course, doesn't make sense with an eclipse in the middle of the day, so we ended up just making it just a function of light."

TOP: Nautiloid concept | Zach Berger and Dylan Cole
ABOVE: Bioluminescent coral concept | Steven Messing
RIGHT: Bioluminescent coral concept | Dylan Cole

THE ECLIPSE

During the development of Pandora, James Cameron came up with the idea of an eclipse season on the moon. With the alignment of the moons and Polyphemus twice a day, there would be an eclipse. Dylan Cole says that for practical reasons, they had to find a balance between physics and what audiences expect an eclipse to look like.

"In our solar system, during an eclipse, it's a bizarre coincidence that our moon and the sun are almost the exact same relative size to us as seen from Earth, when obviously the sizes are vastly different," Cole explains. "That apparent visual size in the sky looks almost identical, so we get this really cool 'diamond ring effect.' In reality, if you have their sun, Alpha Centauri, going behind a gas giant, you're getting pure blackness because it's just blocked out. There's no light leaking around it. Yet we all equate eclipses with that eclipse-y look, so we have a mix. What we were suggesting is that when the sun's coming and going, we get a bit of that diamond ring effect. The argument there is that Polyphemus, the gas giant, has a very thin-yet-active upper atmosphere, so there're a lot of thin gases that can catch the backlight. And then there are different prominences, à la solar flares."

LEFT: **Cove of the Ancestors eclipse concept** | Steven Messing, Dylan Cole
ABOVE: **RDA armada in the eclipse concept** | Dylan Cole

ABOVE: Sling load landing concept | John Park

THE RDA RETURNS

BRIDGEHEAD

In order to be more efficient with its mining and resource missions, the RDA establishes a permanent outpost on Pandora known as Bridgehead. Ben Procter says its geographical and functional footprint is entirely utilitarian. Its massive circular design covers large tracts of real estate across the land and sea and is an imposing visual display of muscle meant to intimidate the Na'vi. Procter says of its design, "Bridgehead's purpose is that of being a construction site. And it's all about humanity implying they're building a whole new city practically overnight. A sort of 'Eff you, *Eywa*.'"

OPPOSITE: Bridgehead map layout concept | Ben Procter, Jonathan Berube

RIGHT: Bridgehead living quarters concept | Fausto De Martini

BELOW: Bridgehead shipyard concept | Ben Procter

BOTTOM: General Ardmore tours Bridgehead concept | Fausto De Martini, John Park

LEFT: Bridgehead construction zone concept | David Levy
BELOW: Bridgehead feedback sketch | James Cameron
BELOW LEFT: Bridgehead warehouse concept | Ben Procter
BELOW RIGHT: Bridgehead wall construction concept | David Levy
BOTTOM LEFT: Parapet wall concept | Andrea Onorato
BOTTOM RIGHT: Seawall closed-gate concept | Shari Ratliff

OPPOSITE: Bridgehead sea gate paint over | Ben Procter, LEI Lab

TOP LEFT: **SeaWasp cockpit concept** | Joe Hiura, Jonathan Berube
TOP RIGHT: **SeaWasp cockpit keyframe** | Jonathan Berube, Joe Hiura
ABOVE: **Tarmac concept** | Fausto De Martini

OPPOSITE: **SeaWasp concept** | Fausto De Martini
OVERLEAF: **Bridgehead Ops Center concept** | Paul Ozzimo, Cantina

SEAWASP

Crafted as a significant upgrade to the Scorpion gunships that preceded it, the SeaWasp is a new-era RDA airship with considerably more agility and lift than those seen in *Avatar*. Ben Procter says their brief for the SeaWasp was to imply that they represent "a generational change of aircraft reflecting the RDA's commitment to taking Pandora on a larger scale. They reflect that we are in the era of F-35 stealthy fighters, not the era of the Huey."

Used primarily for sea-support missions, the exterior coloration is a light metallic gray, which makes it harder for enemies to see during water-based missions. Another way they sought to visually differentiate the gunship was to give it a sleek shape and silhouette. "The SeaWasp is more reminiscent of a fighter jet than a helo," Procter details. "The canopy has a gold coating reminiscent of the F-22 and F-35 fighters. And for the first time, we introduced a conjoined double rotor system on each side of the aircraft."

JAKE

With Jake, his look boils down to everything being functional and having a purpose. "Jake could care less," Scott says, laughing. "He doesn't really change until it is almost forced on him; it's a symbol that he has become part of the Metkayina."

OPPOSITE, TOP LEFT: **Pregnant Neytiri concept** | Steven Messing
OPPOSITE, BOTTOM LEFT: **Neytiri bust** | Legacy Effects
OPPOSITE, BOTTOM MIDDLE: **Neytiri concept** | Joseph C. Pepe
OPPOSITE, RIGHT: **Neytiri costume art** | Wētā Workshop

ABOVE: **Jake costume art** | Wētā Workshop
RIGHT: **Jake battle look costume art** | Wētā Workshop

As a whole, the defining transition for the family in the first act of the film is when the Sully family leaves their home and begins their monumental journey to a new one. They wear specific travel garb for this sequence, and Jake dons a signature poncho.

"Jim would always refer to this as Jake's Clint Eastwood moment because it really establishes character," Scott explains. "It would be one of our first ponchos or capes in our design palette. Jake wore it because as they traveled, they'd need to have something protective. They would need a cape or a cloak to safeguard them from the elements, so it was a purely practical idea. Then it branched off to each of the family and was the gateway to the designs of the capes and capelets that the other Na'vi wear." Scott points out that Spider's cloak is similar to Jake's, once again implying deep connections and emotional bonds.

TOP: **Coastal cliffs concept** | Steven Messing
ABOVE: **Neytiri and child riding an *ikran* sketch** | Keith Christensen
RIGHT: **Neytiri costume concept** | Wētā Workshop

OPPOSITE, TOP LEFT: **Mighty Cliffs windtrader concept** | Steven Messing
OPPOSITE, TOP RIGHT: **Sullys flying to reef** | Dylan Cole
OPPOSITE, MIDDLE LEFT: **Jake's poncho sample** | Wētā Workshop
OPPOSITE, BOTTOM LEFT: **Cloak wardrobe photo** | Wētā Workshop
OPPOSITE, BOTTOM RIGHT: **Jake on *ikran* costume sketch** | Keith Christensen

KIRI

As the Sully family becomes immersed in Metkayinan culture, the costume team introduced more natural-world inspirations into the techniques and materials inherent to this new clan. "One of the primary things that we gravitated to were microscopic images of plants," explains assistant costume designer Hana Scott-Suhrstedt. "Like a lime tree cell or a pinewood cell, so the microscopic is magnified with its connection to *Eywa*. It's this idea that we're all cells—the big, the little, and everything in between—but it doesn't feel scientific to the Na'vi way of thinking. It feels connected and spiritual."

Kiri, in particular, folds that concept into her looks, which organically transitions into her adoption of the Metkayinan ways. "She is the most adaptive to the new culture and environment," Scott assesses. "I say that because Kiri, from the beginning, is a collector.

THIS PAGE: Kiri concept | Legacy Effects

OPPOSITE, LEFT: Kiri bust concept | Legacy Effects
OPPOSITE, RIGHT: Kiri concept | Joseph C. Pepe

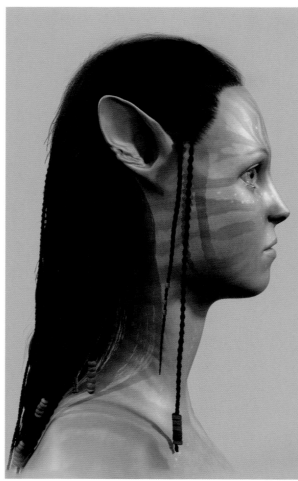

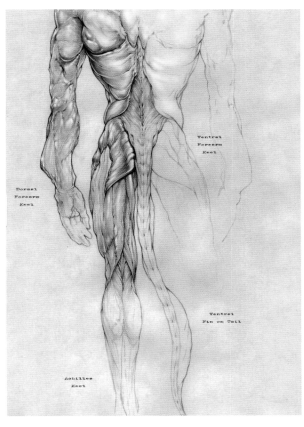

Dorsal
Forearm
Keel

Ventral
Forearm
Keel

Ventral
Fin on Tail

Achilles
Keel

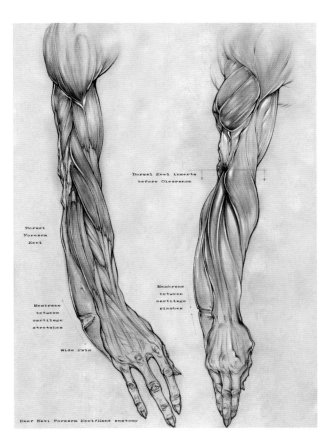

Dorsal Keel inserts
before Olecranon

Dorsal
Forearm
Keel

Membrane
between
cartilage
stretches

Membrane
between
cartilage
pinches

Wide Palm

Reef Navi Forearm Keel/Hand Anatomy

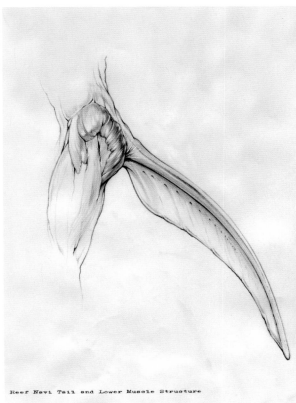

Reef Navi Tail and Lower Muscle Structure

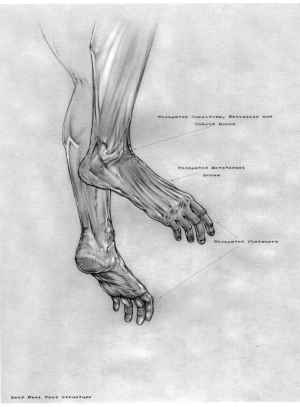

Elongated Cuneiform, Navicular and
Cuboid Bones

Elongated Metatarsal
Bones

Elongated Phalanges

Reef Navi Foot Structure

THE INFLUENCE OF THE SEA

Costume designer Deborah L. Scott began her work on the Metkayina with that detailed description from Cameron, as well as additional notes based on his lifetime of oceanic knowledge and exploration. In particular, he never wanted them to come across as "science-fiction" sea dwellers. He envisioned the Metkayina as being inspired by many communities around our own globe that almost exclusively live near or on the water.

"The reef people have a highly developed aesthetic," Cameron explains. "It's very different than the Omatikaya's aesthetic, although it feels like it's all part of the same general Na'vi aesthetic, which involves curvilinear shapes and spirals and forms that aren't rectilinear. They're not interested in the triangle. They're not interested so much in a circle. They like spirals. They like shapes that weave and flow. They have a very specific aesthetic in a very broad sense, but then we had to come up with what would work for the Metkayina."

With that brief in hand, Scott and her team conducted extensive research, exploring Pacific Islander cultures, which helped establish commonalities among inhabitants of almost every part of the world. "People make things with what they find in their environment, whether it's a plant or an animal or insect," Scott observes. "And these water-adjacent cultures are, in my opinion, very decorative. They like to express themselves with color, with paint, with style. They're not plain."

Invigorated by that knowledge, Scott says they started with a Metkayina color palette that reflected the hues of the ocean reef, the underwater creatures and coral, and in particular, the pāua shell. Found in the waters and on the shores of many oceanfront communities, the interior of the shell informed the foundation of their color realm. "There's no red, and there's no black, but there are a billion other colors that we used very demonstratively," she details. "It also borrowed from the sunsets and sunrises you'd experience on a beach."

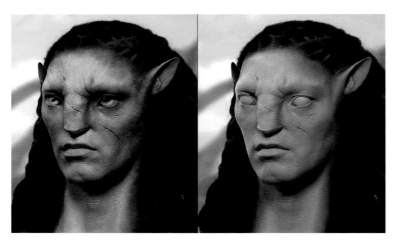

TOP ROW: **Tonowari concept** | Legacy Effects
ABOVE: **Tonowari bust concept** | Joseph C. Pepe
ABOVE RIGHT: **Tonowari, Ronal concept** | Joseph C. Pepe

OPPOSITE, LEFT: **Ronal concept** | Joseph C. Pepe
OPPOSITE, RIGHT: **Tonowari concept** | Joseph C. Pepe
OVERLEAF: **The Sullys meet Tonowari and Ronal concept** | Dylan Cole

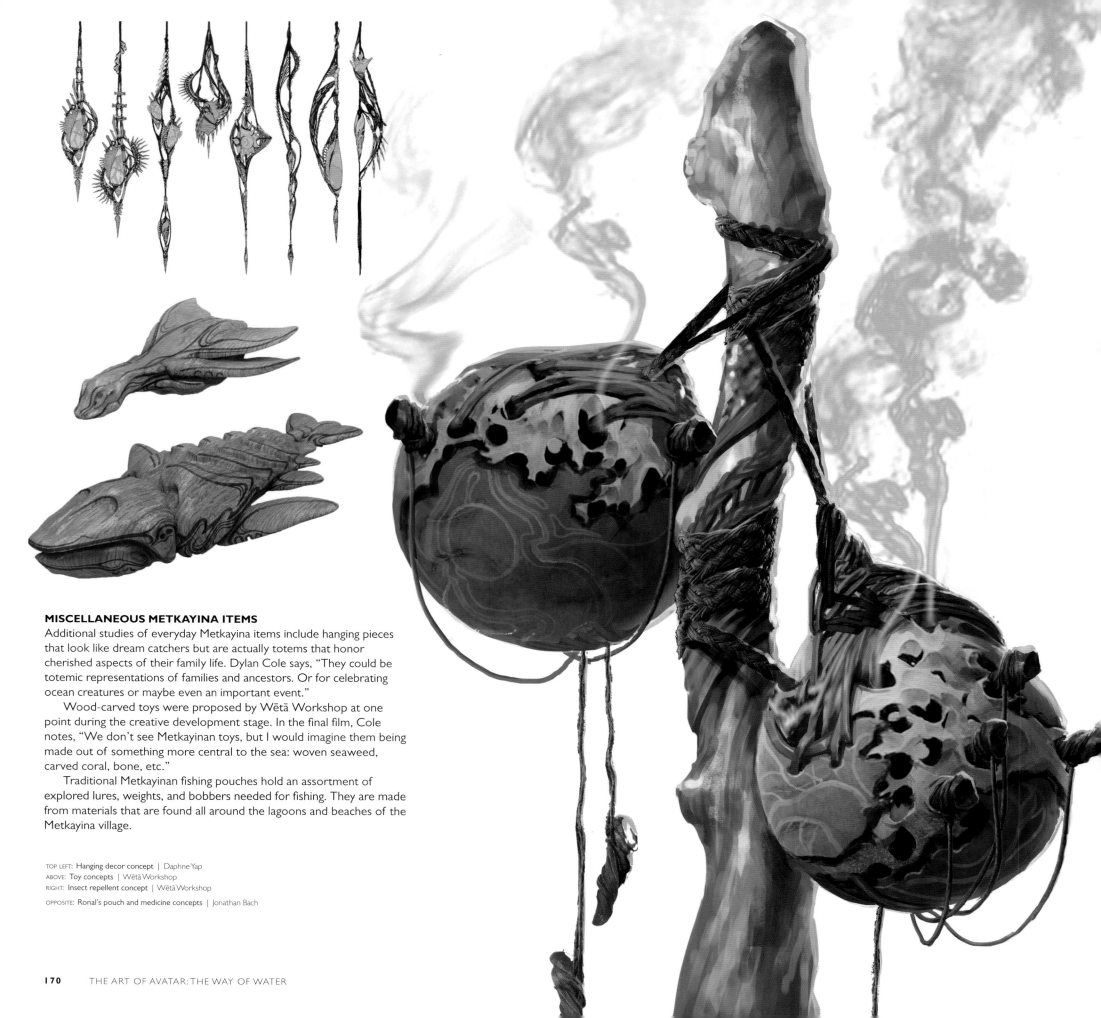

MISCELLANEOUS METKAYINA ITEMS

Additional studies of everyday Metkayina items include hanging pieces that look like dream catchers but are actually totems that honor cherished aspects of their family life. Dylan Cole says, "They could be totemic representations of families and ancestors. Or for celebrating ocean creatures or maybe even an important event."

Wood-carved toys were proposed by Wētā Workshop at one point during the creative development stage. In the final film, Cole notes, "We don't see Metkayinan toys, but I would imagine them being made out of something more central to the sea: woven seaweed, carved coral, bone, etc."

Traditional Metkayinan fishing pouches hold an assortment of explored lures, weights, and bobbers needed for fishing. They are made from materials that are found all around the lagoons and beaches of the Metkayina village.

TOP LEFT: Hanging decor concept | Daphne Yap

ABOVE: Toy concepts | Wētā Workshop

RIGHT: Insect repellent concept | Wētā Workshop

OPPOSITE: Ronal's pouch and medicine concepts | Jonathan Bach

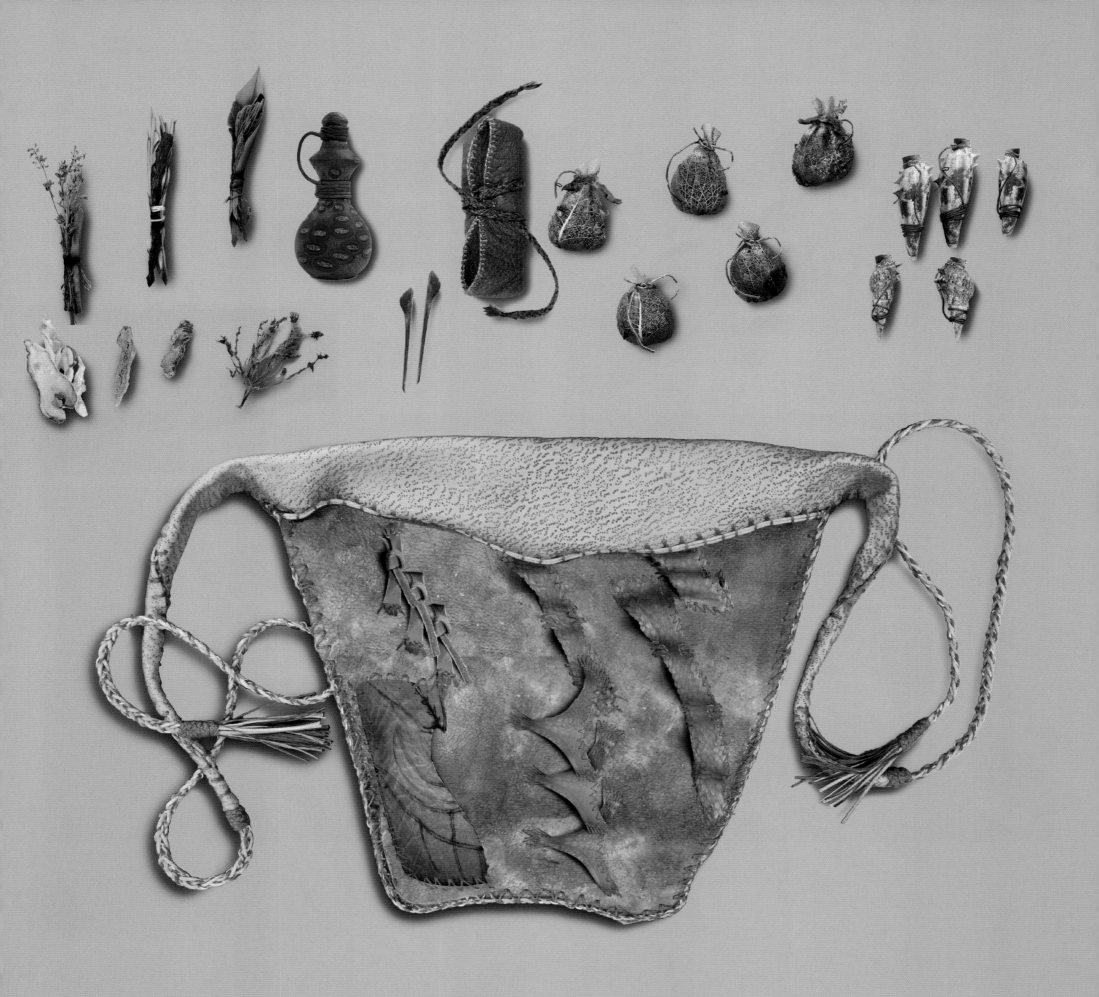

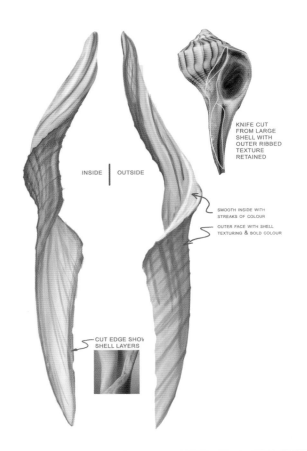

INSIDE | OUTSIDE

KNIFE CUT
FROM LARGE
SHELL WITH
OUTER RIBBED
TEXTURE
RETAINED

SMOOTH INSIDE WITH
STREAKS OF COLOUR

OUTER FACE WITH SHELL
TEXTURING & BOLD COLOUR

CUT EDGE SHOWS
SHELL LAYERS

METKAYINAN KNIVES

The study of Metkayinan knives was led by Deborah L. Scott's team, with collaboration from Dylan Cole's team. A huge design note regarding the knives was to distinguish an Omatikayan style versus a Metkayinan style. Scott explains, "There's a big difference between the materiality of what an Omatikayan knife and a Metkayinan knife look like."

Using an in-world example, costume associate Hana Scott-Suhrstedt poses, "If an Omatikayan kid loses their knife and has to get a new one and they're at the reef, they're going to end up with a knife of a different style. It will be made with different things because they're in an environment where the knife is not going be the same as it was when they were in the forest."

Cole adds, "We continue to use crystal as the primary blade material, and we see the Metkayina's prowess through their intricate woven grips. Colors were pushed compared to the earthier tones Omatikayans favor to show the difference in their cultures."

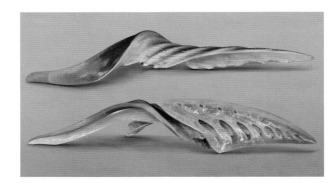

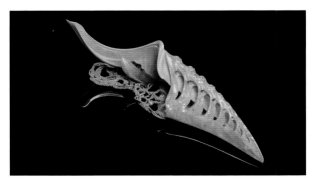

TOP & ABOVE: Ronal ceremonial knife concept and prop design | Wētā Workshop
TOP MIDDLE: Ronal knife color pass concept | Wētā Workshop
TOP RIGHT: Ronal ceremonial knife sample | Wētā Workshop
MIDDLE RIGHT: Ronal crystal knife concept | Wētā Workshop
BOTTOM RIGHT: Ronal crystal knife sample | Wētā Workshop

OPPOSITE, TOP LEFT: Ronal transparent knife concept | Wētā Workshop
OPPOSITE, TOP RIGHT: Ao'nung's knife sample | Wētā Workshop
OPPOSITE, BOTTOM: Tonowari obsidian knife | Wētā Workshop
OVERLEAF: Metkayina funeral concept | Dylan Cole

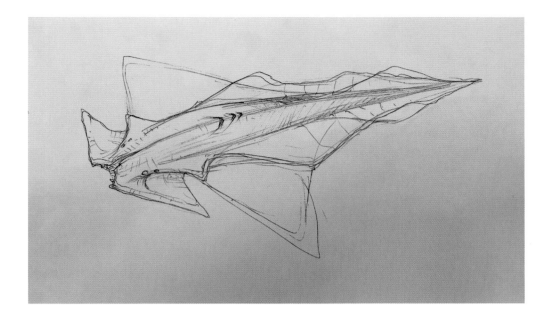

A bona fide playground of marine creature design exists in Pandora's oceans, all brought to life by production designer Dylan Cole, his concept artists, Legacy Effects, and even some ideas provided by Wētā Workshop. Rife with organisms never seen before, the aquatic creations included major set-piece characters like the *ilu* and *tulkun*, all the way down to the newly designed schooling fish.

Throughout his life, Cameron has been an avid scuba diver and a frequent visitor to the depths of the ocean, which has provided him firsthand knowledge of aquatic species both common and rare. He parlayed that intimate knowledge into expansive visuals, creatures, and underwater landscapes that would push Pandora in bold new directions.

Acutely aware of the myriad array of deep-sea creatures in Earth's oceans, which are entirely alien in design and function, Cameron knew that the designers' inherent challenge was besting nature at its own game. "It's pretty hard to come up with something crazier than nature right here on Earth," the director says, laughing.

Because of that, Cole and his artists focused more on using examples from existing nature to create unexpected visual juxtapositions. "Ultimately, you don't want to be so strange that the audience can't buy what they're seeing," Cameron explains.

Based on those parameters, the basic design concept for *Avatar: The Way of Water*'s ecosphere was born: take a real-world structure, shape, or aquatic element and scale it to gigantic proportions. Citing the example of soft gorgonian coral found mainly in the western Atlantic, Cole explains: "It's like an underwater bush probably no more than 18 inches [45.72 cm] tall. But I used several different images and composed it in such a way that it became an underwater tree with a never-ending, forking, coral-type structure."

Using that principal of grounded reinvention, Cole and his team went about creating a broad range of studies so they could ultimately build an underwater playground that is welcoming to both the native sea creatures and the Metkayina, who swim, play, and sustain themselves within its blue waters. The underwater sequences were not only opportunities for the artists to use their creative imaginations, but to create dynamic environments that would inspire the staging for a host of Cameron's marine-based cinematic sequences.

TOP LEFT: Riding *ilu* through the reef | John Park
TOP RIGHT: *Ilu* chatters at Lo'ak concept | Jonathan Berube
LEFT: *Ilu* with Metkayina child | Legacy Effects
ABOVE: Fish concept | Constantine Sekeris

TULKUN

"The *tulkun* are not creatures; they are an intelligent species, some of whom are actual characters in the films," Landau explains. Aside from the reef village, Cole says the *tulkun* was probably the biggest design challenge for *A2*. "It went through so many designs because it's very much written as a whale and functions as a whale. But how whalelike do you make it?"

An important species to get right, Cameron concurs that zeroing in on what the *tulkun* needed to look like became an unexpectedly lengthy and fraught process. "I felt we were struggling to keep the essence of what you'd immediately recognize as a whale, yet the specific details had to be very alien. The example that I used for the artists was the direhorse. You look at it and it's clearly a horse. But when you really get to study it, it is some strange, alien dinosaur that has some horselike properties. I wanted the same thing with the *tulkun*. There should be no doubt in your mind

what the metaphor is, but the specifics of it are very alien and strange, and totally unique to that species."

Cameron was so dissatisfied with the *tulkun* explorations at one point that he took it upon himself to sketch out some ideas. "We had so many different *tulkun* designs, and some of them were quite interesting," he shares. "But none of them were quite hitting what I thought was the essence of it. I broke that piece off myself, and I holed up for a day and a half. I did around 20 sketches until I finally focused in on what I wanted." He gave the sketches to Cole, who used them to hone new designs with Ian Joyner and Constantine Sekeris leading the way, with Zach Berger doing final tweaks. "They went through many iterations from Jim's illustrations. And then it all slowly and steadily came into focus." Cole says the creature made a full-circle journey from very alien-looking back to the familiar lines and silhouette of a whale by the time the final *tulkun* design was approved.

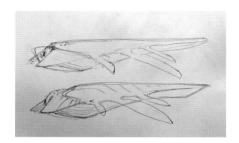

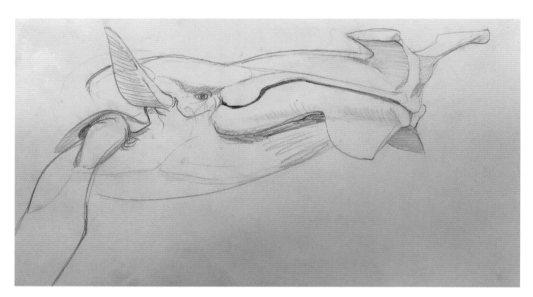

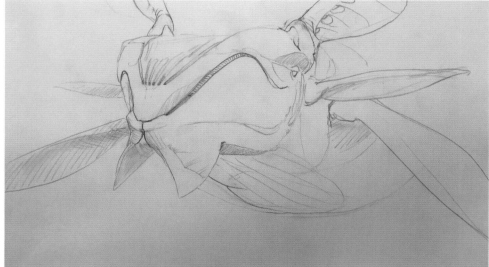

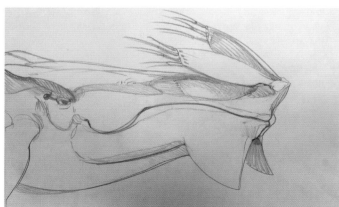

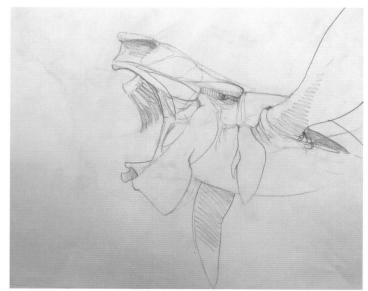

TOP RIGHT: *Tulkun* sketch | Constantine Sekeris
ABOVE ROWS: *Tulkun* sketches | James Cameron

OPPOSITE, TOP LEFT: Lo'ak signing to Payakan concept | Zach Berger
OPPOSITE, TOP RIGHT: Lo'ak riding Payakan concept | Zach Berger
OPPOSITE, BOTTOM: *Tulkun* mother and calf concept | Ian Joyner

GILL MANTLE

A concept unique to *A2* is the gill mantle. Cameron conceived of this as an organic organism that latches to the back of a Metkayina via their *kuru*. "Basically, it's an organic scuba apparatus," Dylan Cole clarifies. "Jim wanted something diaphanous and beautiful. Legacy Effects did some beautiful early designs, but some looked a little too invasive, and we joked that it was too similar to the face hugger from *Alien*. And then creature designer Ian Joyner was doing some cool stuff where it was starting to get a little bit more diaphanous and beautiful, almost like a piece of wardrobe. It was a ray-meets-jellyfish thing that would swim in a very sinusoidal movement. That led to Constantine Sekeris's final design."

After going through many iterations, Cole says it eventually evolved into an elegant design with little sucker feet. "Jim talked about gecko feet to hold onto the ribs so that you believe that it's latched on. And that was needed because some of our characters are going quickly, whether they're riding an *ilu* or swimming fast."

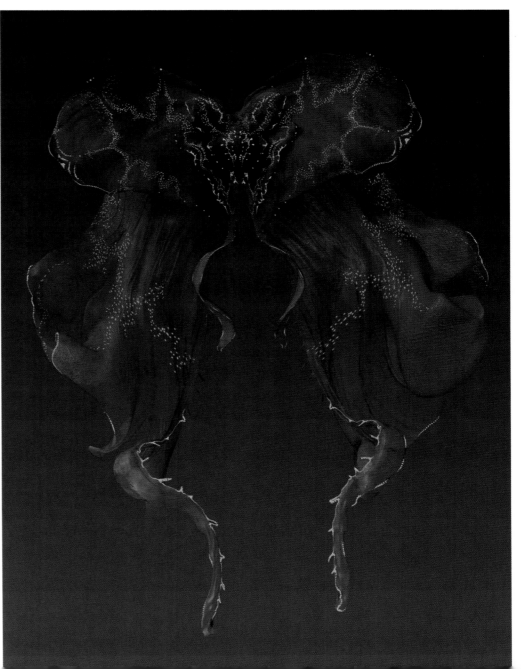

ABOVE: Gill mantle concept | Daphne Yap
MIDDLE RIGHT: Kiri with gill mantle concept | Constantine Sekeris
TOP RIGHT: Kiri with squids concept | Jonathan Bach
FAR RIGHT: Gill mantle bioluminescent patterns concept | Daphne Yap

FISH STUDIES

Looking to fill the Pandoran oceans with a plethora of exotic yet slightly familiar riffs on recognizable fish, Dylan Cole's creature designers, especially Zach Berger and Constantine Sekeris, did countless passes on everything from baitfish, also called schooling fish, to more distinctive species. "We did a lot of these baitfish, asking how we can make these different," Cole says. "We ended up playing with the idea that they're still basically torpedoes, but we just added crazy fun tail fins onto very simple shapes."

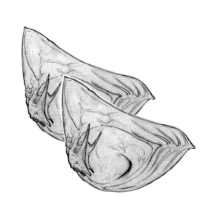

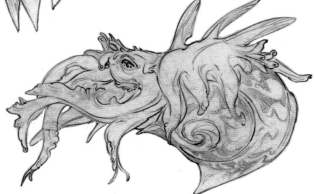

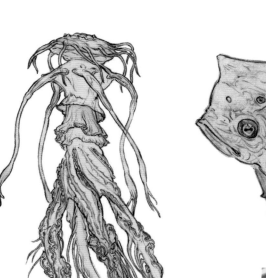

ABOVE: Sea creature sketches | Daphne Yap
TOP ROWS: Fish sketches | Daphne Yap
RIGHT: *Ilu* and daggerbeak feeding in a baitball | Dylan Cole

OPPOSITE, TOP ROW: Fish sketches | James Cameron
OPPOSITE, SECOND ROW: Hammer brow (Constantine Sekeris); pincher, syringil (Zach Berger)
OPPOSITE, THIRD ROW: Flat skate (Zach Berger), chandelier, starbeak (Zach Berger, Legacy Effects)
OPPOSITE, BOTTOM ROW: spade wing (Zach Berger, Ian Joyner), angel sperm (Constantine Sekeris), feather tail (Zach Berger)

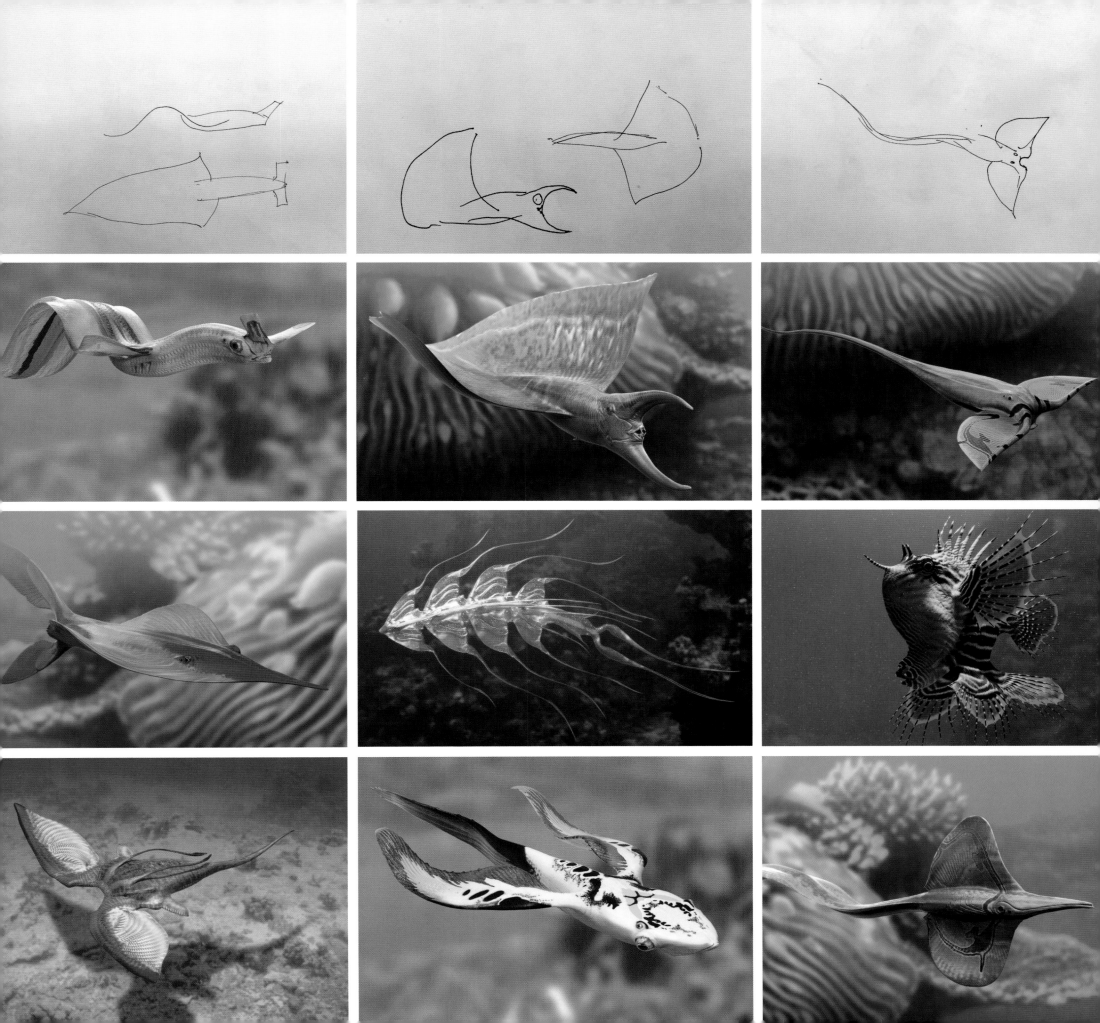

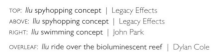
TOP: *Ilu* spyhopping concept | Legacy Effects
ABOVE: *Ilu* spyhopping concept | Legacy Effects
RIGHT: *Ilu* swimming concept | John Park

OVERLEAF: *Ilu* ride over the bioluminescent reef | Dylan Cole

AKULA

"Jim said that the *akula* is essentially the Pandoran equivalent of a great white," Cole recalls. "He originally gravitated toward a cool, simple body plan design by Wētā Workshop. But we needed to explore the design of the head. Zach Berger, one of our creature guys, started running with it and took the concept through many ideas unto completion.

"One thing we do a lot is surprise transformations; for example, creature heads where a frill pops out, or something extra that's unexpected. Jim wanted elements like a great white, where it opens its mouth and you see those crazy gums and teeth. We looked at a side snapper, as well as a three-part mouth as found on a rattlesnake. We didn't integrate the separation of the jaw, but we did for the top of the mouth, only with a hard-ish palette. It's bifurcated down the middle and can spread outward. Jim ultimately went with the rattlesnake head option because of it being able to claw through coral easier. We also liked the idea of it feeling more like a snake when you see it attacking its prey. Jim pared it down to be more sharklike, but we put some cooler, simple stripes and some patterning on it. We also have a little hint of color going down the side."

TOP COLUMN: *Akula* concepts | Zach Berger
ABOVE & RIGHT: *Akula* attacks Lo'ak and his *ilu* | Dylan Cole
OVERLEAF: **Three Brothers concept** | Nick Gindraux, Dylan Cole

MATADOR

There are also the lethal aspects to the RDA's boats. Fitted to the bow of the Matador vessels are heavy-duty harpoon launchers that are integral to *tulkun* hunts. Procter says they examined real harpoon guns used for whaling for inspiration. "We looked at the latest in motorized 30 mm shipboard gun turrets, as well as older models that are directly crew-operated. The use of a bright red color is reminiscent of industrial equipment and also suggests the machine's murderous purpose. The final design is complete with two HUDs and a radial track attaching it to the boat, which hopefully transcends all the reference to become its own unique, badass weapon of RDA cruelty."

The character of Mick Scoresby (Brendan Cowell) is a primary operator of the harpoon gun, and Procter says they created shoulder stocks so he could be fully engaged with his weapon of expertise. "He's almost integrated into it as he pivots with the gun in his platform and hugs the grips to him."

TOP: Matador harpoon concept | Fausto De Martini, Liam Beck
ABOVE: Matador harpoon concept | Joe Hiura, Jonathan Berube
RIGHT: Matador whaling formation concept | Fausto De Martini, Liam Beck

PICADOR

The Picador would also require a variety of bespoke weapons for herding the giant marine mammals by depth-charge grenade and sonic projection. "Riot control speakers were a key reference for the sound cannon," Procter shares, "but Jim wanted an exciting, evocative shape and sketched a trilateral configuration that worked well." The grenade launcher's munitions were scaled up to 90mm to be powerful enough for their job.

A unique and exciting challenge with the Picador was Cameron's demand that the 32-foot (9.75-m) boat be built as a practical running picture vehicle. Art director and naval architect Alister Baxter took on the refinement of the design into a proper, ground-up boat, which he equipped with 1,000HP engines and dual HamiltonJet drives, propelling the athletic, wave-jumping craft to over 40 knots (46mph / 74kph).

LEFT: Depth charge grenade launcher concept | Fausto De Martini
BELOW LEFT: Sound cannon concept | NZ Props, Mat Hunkin
BOTTOM LEFT: Picador stern view concept | Alister Baxter, Liam Beck
BELOW: Picador photo composite | Alister Baxter, Ben Procter
BOTTOM RIGHT: Picador cockpit layout | Alister Baxter, Liam Beck

OPPOSITE, TOP: Firing depth charges from Picador concept | Jonathan Bach, Ben Procter
OPPOSITE, BOTTOM: Rescue variant concept | Jonathan Berube, Alister Baxter, LEI Lab

RECOMS

When it comes to their plan to take back Pandora, one of Earth's new strategic tools is the RDA's Recom Program. It expands on tech from the Avatar Program to create autonomous recombinant avatars using RDA-programmed DNA of soldiers like Quaritch instead of more passive scientists such as Norm Spellman (Joel David Moore).

"They're like the Special Forces," says costume designer Deborah L. Scott of the Recom's real-world military inspiration. "They have their own progression and start off, supposedly, much more regimented." However, she says it was tricky to figure out what would look natural and realistic when dressing 9-foot- (2.74-meter-) tall blue people as soldiers. "We were basically making things to human scale, but as their body shape was so different, having to fully clothe them created a proportion issue. Everyone was trying to adapt to the scale, asking how big is this knife or how big is that gun? It's a different kind of problem because other costumes, like the loincloths, could fit anybody." In figuring out how to make those details work, Scott and her team worked on the general aesthetics, but it was eventually exploring individualization that finally cracked the Recom problem.

LEFT: Quaritch speech in Squad Bay keyframe | Ben Procter
ABOVE: Recom Mansk concept | Wētā Workshop

"The Recoms really bridge the humans and Na'vi," Scott clarifies. Because of that, she and her team had to home in on and reflect the similarities and the differences between the two. "What really defined the soldiers were their hairstyles and their tattoos, because those are much more human-based constructs."

Scott and production designer Ben Procter worked together to create cohesive designs that also blended with the RDA graphics. "The insignia patch for the Recoms was influenced by Stephen Lang," Scott reveals. "Because it's his troop and his guys, he was really into it. He gave it the name, and we went back and forth with some designs and got his and Jim's approval."

A lot of designs for the soldiers' tattoos and other distinguishing artworks were created and then presented to Cameron for review. During one review process, Cameron asked for a unique female Recom, Zdinarsk (Alicia Bailey), who would sport a Mohawk and color tattoos. "We went back in and put color on her, and that was pretty fun," she enthuses. "There're some really intricate and well-thought-out tattoos across the whole group."

Along with the Recoms is an entire cavalcade of military hardware designed to aid their new mission. Procter's mandate in creating all of it was to design for every reasonable possibility. "In Jim's mind, he wants everything he puts on screen to look as if it were real," he explains. "And, in some ways, it is real. Therefore, the challenge for all of us on the hard surface team was to immerse ourselves in the future of the RDA. What would it really do? And what would it be like to be there, surrounded by this immensely expensive equipment, very much like the real extraction industries of the world?"

HUMAN SKULL
Adorned with Quaritch's treble-scar, the skull represents the death of the human soldier.

NA'VI SKULL
The Na'vi skull represents the soldier's rebirth as a more powerful warrior. The lion-like canine teeth and pointed ear denote the soldier's transformation into an alpha predator.

SNAKE QUEUE
The Na'vi skull's plaited queue morphs into a snake as it descends, a symbol of cunning and death. It also evokes the danger of the jungle environment.

MACHETE
The bushwhacking machete symbolises the Recom unit's expertise in jungle warfare.

OPPOSITE, LEFT: **Deja Blu patch design** | Wētā Workshop
OPPOSITE, RIGHT: **Quaritch costume concept** | Wētā Workshop
RIGHT: **Quaritch concept** | Legacy Effects
BELOW, BOTTOM & FAR RIGHT: **Wainfleet concept** | Legacy Effects

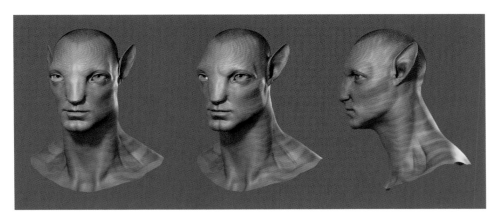

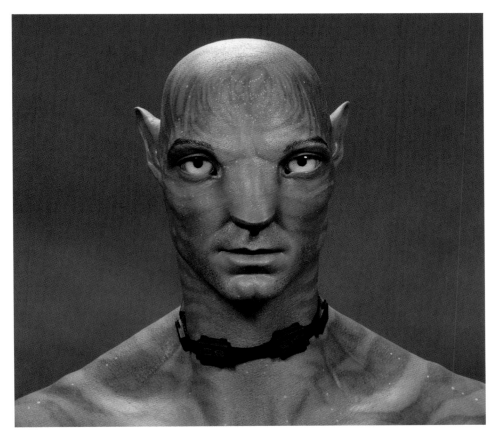

ABOVE: Zdinarsk tattoos concept | Wētā Workshop

TOP RIGHT: Zdinarsk chimera tattoo design | Wētā Workshop

MIDDLE RIGHT: Zdinarsk eagle tattoo design | Wētā Workshop

RIGHT: Zdinarsk left and right sleeve tattoo designs | Wētā Workshop

TOP LEFT: Fike panther tattoo design | Wētā Workshop
MIDDLE FAR LEFT: Vulture tattoo design | Wētā Workshop
BOTTOM FAR LEFT: Giddy Up tattoo design | Wētā Workshop

LEFT: Trench knife tattoo design | Wētā Workshop
ABOVE: Fike tattoo concept | Wētā Workshop